WINNING
at BEING You

Seated In Your Rightful Place

DR. JOHN D. MCCONNELL

AuthorHouse™
1663 Liberty Drive
Bloomington, IN 47403
www.authorhouse.com
Phone: 833-262-8899

Because of the dynamic nature of the Internet, any web addresses or links contained in this book may have changed since publication and may no longer be valid. The views expressed in this work are solely those of the author and do not necessarily reflect the views of the publisher, and the publisher hereby disclaims any responsibility for them.

Any people depicted in stock imagery provided by Getty Images are models, and such images are being used for illustrative purposes only.
Certain stock imagery © Getty Images.

This book is printed on acid-free paper.

ISBN: 979-8-8230-2455-6 (sc)
ISBN: 979-8-8230-2456-3 (e)

Library of Congress Control Number: 2024907614

Print information available on the last page.

Published by AuthorHouse 04/30/2024

authorHOUSE®

Contents

DEDICATION

This book is dedicated to everyone who has ever felt worthless. If you have ever felt like your dreams don't matter, this book is dedicated to you. If you've been unable to figure out how to finish the things you've started, this is your book. There is a kindred spirit amongst those who share unique experiences. We don't always get a chance to meet face-to-face, but this book is our meeting ground. You are not weird, worthless, or inadequate. You're still evolving into who you shall be. I meet some of you within every venue I attend, and it's gratifying to know that I am not alone in my pursuit for my best life. To everyone who has felt like an outcast, and that you should quit - don't do it! Your happiness, wholeness, and true destiny is contingent upon your fight. Allow the words of this book to fan the flames of your passion to win at being you!

INTRODUCTION

I am a Christian author. Any example, anecdote, or analogy used in this book presupposes God as Lord.

The Throne is often referred to as 'the office of the ruler'. Monarchs — kings and queens — sit on thrones on special ceremonial occasions, and so do religious figures such as bishops and popes. It represents the power of the dignitary who sits on it and sometimes confers that power.

Imagine your life as your kingdom (where you reside). There is a hierarchy within your kingdom, which should have you seated in the king's chair. This seat represents your kingdom's chain of command. It's not only about how others see you, but how you see yourself. Power flows down from the head, and if anyone is elevated above you (in your kingdom) - your life is out of order. It's time you take back the throne by unlocking the door to your true identity. You can't be your absolute best without first knowing who you are.

Usually, we read books through the filter of the author's accomplishments. We tend to qualify or disqualify the message based on the popularity of the vessel. Although I do draw from some personal experiences in this book, I make a valiant effort to distance myself from your results. If you truly work certain principles, the outcomes should have no bearing on the messenger. I debated using this title, "Winning At Being You", for a long time because of the connotation of the word 'winning'. Traditionally, when someone speaks of winning, their backdrop displays jets, mansions, luxury cars, and private islands. Not many people would argue that these things don't represent winning. But why do some people who can live extravagant lifestyles, spiral in depression or commit suicide? It's because our definition of rich and wealthy doesn't include being whole. It's broader than a financial portfolio. When a person learns how to investigate who they really are, that's the beginning of truly winning! We've been strapped in way too long. Unbuckle your seatbelt and take this journey with me.

CHAPTER 1

MANAGING YOUR CHOICES

Life isn't a race, but at times it feels very competitive. Who's the opponent? Who is the perceived threat contending for what I'm after? Is it a person? Is it a window of time? Am I chasing an idea, and if so, how did it get lodged in my thinking? We live in a very complicated world that increasingly becomes more difficult to navigate because of unlimited choices. I know you're thinking, "I love having choices". Yes, choices are great to have, but they can also be very suffocating. When I go into a store looking for skin care lotion, I must sift through several rows of products that offer different claims similar to my actual need. If there are five items on my shopping list, multiply this experience by five. Too many choices!

When we are children, it's important for us to have adults tell us we can become anything we choose. That affirmation is crucial when you're still establishing self-worth. There is a deeper truth within that affirmation. It's not a guarantee just because you've decided to want it. Even after fulfilling the checklist of character, skill, tenacity, ability, education, experience, etc. - you still may not qualify. While reading these pages, examine why you want what you want. Once we've thoroughly had this debate with ourselves, we can move into a phase called "permission". This is when we stop chasing the illusion of who we are, and begin running towards who we see in the mirror.

Seated in Your Rightful Place

PUT IN THE WORK!

After 29 years of marriage, I experienced divorce. The separation between my wife and I lasted nearly 6 years before I finally realized divorce was inevitable. Someone else walked into my life and made my heart leap with enthusiasm. I began to really enjoy her personality, laugh, warmth, and genuine concern for me as a friend. My brain said to me, "You could easily start a new life with her". In my imagination, I could see myself starting over with her. That was the start of something totally new for me. The realization that I could be happy with someone else brought the clarity I needed. But I was in no position to approach her (and be taken seriously). I didn't want to have a story about how I one day would be getting a divorce. I wanted to approach her with "clean hands". How dare a married man romantically pursue a new relationship, toting a story of an impending divorce? I didn't want to be that guy, so that's when the road to divorce began for me. When my wife first started talking to me about her thoughts of moving into her own apartment, I remember constructing contingency plans in my mind. I thought, "If she leaves, I'm going to change the locks and forbid her to ever enter the house again". I was angry, and I wanted to respond to her hurting me by hurting her. Based on how other men I knew responded to this type of situation, and movies I'd seen - I had calculated my response. When she did follow through and elected to move out, my conscience wouldn't allow me to be "that guy". Oh, I wanted to be him so bad (inflicting pain for pain), but my God-consciousness posed me with questions. Will responding that way bring healing to the situation? Would I prefer my 15 and 13-year- old sons to see me respond to their mother with grace or wrath? So, I didn't change the locks or deny her access to her children. I didn't cuss her out or dishonor her to her sons. I felt penalized at times for choosing the high road, but of course that wasn't unexpected. We're in a much better place now, which allows us to parent our now adult children with more civility - but getting here demanded intense work. Just so you know, my story didn't end up like in the movies - I didn't get the girl. Although our interests weren't exactly aligned, she was a reminder of feelings I had completely forgotten. And that was enough to force my life to reset. I'm no longer chasing "the girl", but the beautiful, expansive, colorful, exciting life she represents. Who or what needs to enter your life to disrupt your 'holding pattern' of stagnation? Are you delaying shaking up something you've already recognized as inevitable in your life because of the amount of work you know it will take? This is not where I try to make you feel good. Yes, it's going to cost you royally, because change involves shedding people, systems, behaviors, attitudes, and anger. Many would agree that anger prevented necessary conversations, interventions, and solutions that could have fostered more positive resolutions in their life from occurring. Cooler heads usually prevail, and bad habits don't just go away. The guarantee you seek will come from the work you invest in winning back your life!

Seated in Your Rightful Place

<u>WHO ARE YOU?</u>

I know you don't want to label yourself, but if you don't, others will. Your perception of who you are must be the most dominant.

Truthfulness starts with being honest with yourself. I've learned there are a plethora of ways to justify procrastination. You may call it something other than procrastination, but whenever there's a continuous cycle of delay in your output - call a spade a spade. Be truthful and answer the question. What's causing you to not move out into being the happiest version of you? Have you taken the time to discover what makes you truly happy? I know that sounds strange, but many people have submitted their lives into other people for so long, and have forgotten who they used to be. Submitting your life is far different than partnering your life. When you submit, you place yourself underneath. I was raised in church, and I agree with what the bible says in Ephesians 5:22 - 24. Paraphrased, these scriptures instruct wives to submit themselves to their husbands – whom God has delegated 'head of household'. This is not to be confused with the establishment of order. Husbands and wives should operate in partnership with one another. However, when agreement cannot occur, God's hierarchy establishes the husband as the tiebreaker. The point I want to magnify is to work arm and arm, not from a posture of being underneath. It's time to take a retreat - intentionally isolate yourself to rediscover what you really want in life. Unless you're honest with yourself, most everything you do is a lie. I'm not labeling you or attempting to be harsh, but you may not realize that all responses are conditioned.

Honesty also demands us to be transparent about what we don't know. Just because people aren't aware that you haven't mastered a specific thing - it doesn't make you any less vulnerable. In fact, you're subject to experience greater harm from denial. For example, you've always seen ads about purchasing virus protection software for your computer, but you never took the time to learn the relevance of internet

Seated in Your Rightful Place

security. Your choosing not to secure your family's private information, makes you an easy target for identity theft and other internet scams. It's the world we live in. It's not fair, but we're responsible for what we don't know. Instead of ignoring things we don't understand, begin surrounding yourself with a network of people who'll keep you plugged in.

Society often portrays false narratives. In the marketing world, advertisement executives create an idea, then develop strategies to entice potential consumers to internalize it. Once we begin repeating it, rehearsing it, drinking it, eating it, seeing it, it shifts into being something we embrace. Just like products, the same is true of people. Avenues for sharing, such as social media, have made it a simple process to send messages of who we are. The problem is, very little of it must be true, and once we begin fabricating, it never ends. Aren't you tired of living a lie? Let yourself off the hook. Don't just share factual accounts of your journey. Actually live your life! There's no one like you in the world!

Seated in Your Rightful Place

CHAPTER 2

RECOGNIZE YOUR TRIGGERS

Blaming others will never afford us the success we desire. Even if we perceive that someone is blocking our path, everything we experience is necessary. Just as critical as the butterfly making its own metamorphosis from the cocoon, or the baby chick pecking for freedom from the eggshell - pushing through barriers is what qualifies us mentally to withstand physically. Learn to recognize triggers that cause massive delays, and employ strategies to push beyond them. To assign blame is to give away power, and we need as much of that as we can get. Meaningful strategies allow you to tap into power no one can take from you. It's important to accept that "delay" will always be part of our journey. Learning to wait for rewards is beneficial. Just make sure the delay you're experiencing is part of the process, and not due to your inability to appropriately respond to a situation.

Are you trying to make certain things happen because you've been told you can't do it? That's not at all a winning strategy. Proving people wrong is a game you can't win. I don't mean that it's unlikely that you will show up your naysayers - but that's an improper fuel source. It's an awesome feeling to be right, but it's so much more rewarding to be right because of your mission. Be careful if you find that you are being energized by opposition. A goal-oriented person should not require an external stimulus in order to be productive.

Any documentary ever made about the late Kobe Bryant spends time highlighting how he seemed to radiate from the energy of the opposing teams' disdain for him. The louder he was heckled by the crowd, the fiercer opponent he became. Kobe's mission to win was never in question, but his campaign to embarrass teams was elevated by the sneers of his opposition. You may not always have to be the underdog in your pursuit of your dreams. So learn to focus on the obstacle that's immediately in front of you, rather than relying on contributing factors to intensify your resolve.

Listening and hearing are two different things. Your ability to repeat back to someone what they just told you, doesn't mean you truly heard what they said. How I attend to your words in my follow-through is the litmus test for whether I've comprehended what you said at all. Hearing involves more than the ears - the heart must enter in. When the heart is involved in a conversation, the words are like vines - latching on securely to a welcoming host. It's impossible not to care once you establish emotional attachments. Your ability to internalize information is greatly determined by your connection to it. If you typically keep people a certain distance away from you, it only makes sense that the bonds

Seated in Your Rightful Place

you'll form won't be close. I understand that conventional wisdom dictates that we set boundaries. So how do we decide who gets to be close? Unfortunately, there's not a one-size-fits-all answer to that question. It's a difficult task, but we are all responsible for the relationships we nurture.

What people think of you is important, but not ultimately. People see us and think about who we remind them of - which suggests they don't see us as an original. I don't want to be a copy of someone else, so most certainly I don't want to be limited by someone's expectations of me (or lack thereof). I know this is shocking, but many people can't fathom you as a success. Imagining you as a CEO totally disrupts their psyche, so how can they assign an original perspective to you? They can't. So move away from needing the approval of others just to be who you already are. You're already you. I'm just encouraging you to win at it!

What I desired as a teenager is much different than what I desire now. Experience is a great teacher. Every lesson doesn't end with maturity, but once you've gone down a road several times, you begin to sense what's ahead. If you don't like what you've been getting, change your route. There's absolutely nothing wrong with reassessing your plan. However, it's vital that your plan is based on substance. Never overlook considerations you have. The very concerns you disregard along the way, will confront you at the most inopportune times. Get to know yourself really well so you're not easily chased off your own decisions. Knowing what you want with absolution gives you strength to fortify your stance on how you believe. As we grow older and reflect, all of those experiences should inform any plans we make going forward.

Most jobs require their employees to take a personality assessment from time to time (Myers-Briggs, Eysenck Personality Questionnaire, True Colors, etc.). Although there is no exact predictor of behavior, these are great tools to give us a sense of the character traits we display most

Seated in Your Rightful Place

often. If I have a tendency to make most decisions based on emotions, I should definitely know that about myself - as well as any other patterns I may have.

How do you know if it's time to abandon one plan for another? Yet another question with not just one simple answer. So much is tied to who we are and where we're headed. Without a doubt, every successful pursuit of oneself must include passion, purpose, and fulfillment. If your current trajectory is missing any of these, I suggest you take the nearest exit - because you're chasing someone else's dream.

Passion - Purpose - Fulfillment

This definition implies a tug-of-war. If I have passion for something or someone, I am emotionally invested - perhaps even to the degree of over compromising myself. This emotion causes me to stay longer than I probably should, or say yes, when red flags are telling me I should say no. Passion makes a great teammate, but as a solo act, it will bankrupt you.

pas•sion

noun

Strong and barely controllable emotion

pur•pose

noun

The reason for which something is done or created, or for which something exists

Purpose is when you understand what you were born to accomplish. Dr Myles Monroe said, "When purpose is not known, abuse is inevitable". People, money, inventions, and words have specific outcomes encoded in their creative design to produce. When purpose is obstructed, depression occurs.

Seated in Your Rightful Place

To be concise, fulfillment is about having more than you currently possess. No one has the right to tell you that you have everything you need, even if it's true.

ful•fill•ment

noun

The achievement of something desired, promised, or predicted

Some will never arrive at this place. Even when we locate the treasure map for fulfillment, launch the expedition, and excavate the loot, somehow, it won't be the prize we imagined. Like desires, promises, and predictions, how we perceive our own fulfillment changes.

Seated in Your Rightful Place

CHAPTER 3

LIVING WITH THE CONSEQUENCE

We typically understand that there is a judgment for everything we do. Water your plants and they'll grow. Brush your teeth daily to maintain good oral hygiene. It's only when we view the responses to our actions as negative, that we classify them as consequences. Being late to work because you forgot to set your alarm is just as much a consequence as your car engine seizing, due to a lack of oil. Both are your fault and solely your responsibility. One costs you more than the other, but they are consequences one in the same. What do you call it when something good follows your behavior, like getting a perfect score on an exam you studied for? Just because it's a positive action yielding a positive outcome, it doesn't change that it's still a consequence. Remaining true to one's character comes with sacrifice. Sometimes how you feel about your actions are the consequences you must learn to live with. Trading honesty and integrity has a huge price tag that many don't consider during the transaction. As you're adorning your vision board, be sure the choices you make for what you want agree with your character.

Winning at who you are requires your authenticity. Having mentors is important, but be careful not to emulate them. If an individual, organization, or situation doesn't extract the best from you, examine your connection. Your ability to be fully present hinges on everything that influences your life. Hanging on to situations beyond their usefulness can be extremely detrimental to growth. Am I telling you to throw away people? I would never encourage someone to abandon a healthy, nurturing relationship - but at times we must reassign the roles people play in our lives. The world doesn't need the diluted version of you. To make your indelible mark on the world, labor to be full strength. We essentially rob the world of a gift when we fail to do the work of uncovering our true identity.

Winning in life is not only measured by my passion, purpose, and fulfillment - but also by what I give voice to in the world. We all must "choose our battles", but there are some battles that choose us. When it's of significance, do you offer an opinion? On issues that directly affect your community, do you lend your voice? As you're discovering how to champion your life, consider whether you want to be a passive bystander, or support for a cause. Getting involved and standing for something feels good. It doesn't even require you to be aggressive. Simply begin being the solution to the problems you see. I have what I call a "store parking lot ministry". Most of the time when I arrive at a grocery store, there are shopping carts throughout the parking lot. Sometimes parking spaces are blocked because

Seated in Your Rightful Place

of the carts. I usually grab one on my way into the store since I'll probably use it anyway. And after shopping, exiting the store and transferring my groceries, I take the same cart back inside. I know that's only one shopping cart, but what if everyone got involved? Here's the essence of my sharing this story. One day, my oldest son who is now twenty-four was driving me home following an appointment. He decided to stop by a grocery store for a few items. After parking the car and hopping out, guess what he did next? He grabbed a shopping cart from the parking lot on his way inside. I wonder where he learned that. The empowerment we give doesn't have to always be verbal. You're being watched, so make it count!

Grace

A consequence of living a life of Godliness, is grace. I receive upgrades, perks, discounts, and rewards simply by having a relationship with God. Although grace is God's unmerited favor towards me, it's consequential, because He calls me friend. Grace perpetuates grace. If you're not comfortable with this word, substitute it for "giving". It's a proven principle that when you give to others, it comes back to you. If it seems people are never kind to you, 'check your fruit'. Why would Jesus caution us to, 'do unto others, as we would have them do unto us' (Matthew 7:12), if the consequence were not real? Whatever you want to experience more of, begin sowing that into the lives of others.

If you truly feel there are voids (gaps, holes) in your life where something significant is missing, change your routine. Some encounter must get you to that place of revelation - when the alarms go off and your eyes are opened, unlike ever before. I can't tell you what it will take or who you'll need to meet - but

Seated in Your Rightful Place

when it happens, you'll experience peace in a whole new way. Some may debate me on this, but KNOWING what to chase can feel just as remarkable as HAVING it. Statistics support that most children grow up to work in the same occupation as one of their parents. From the time we are toddlers, we begin emulating the actions of our caregivers. Even when our parents complain about their careers, they somehow subconsciously guide us into traveling that path. Unless there's a deliberate interruption, plan, or strategy to move us in a different direction, more than likely we're joining the family business. If perhaps 'the family business' is not God's purpose for your life, it may provide financial stability, but what about being whole (happy, productive, inspired, excited)? There is joyful anticipation in knowing what you're going after.

Seated in Your Rightful Place

KNOWING VS NOT KNOWING

- Gives me a point of focus
- Allows me to be honest with myself
- Allows me to see the prize I am pursuing
- As I get closer, the more fulfilled I become

- Aimless Endeavors
- Causes me to make excuses
- Leaves me frustrated and confused
- No gauge for determining how much further to go

The biggest consequence of all to live with is learning that there is no finish line. Once you have attained that dream for your life, I don't believe it's possible to shut off the valve. If your actions are decent and kind, there's no such thing as having too much. If we are truly excited to be the difference, slowing down or stopping is futile.

Seated in Your Rightful Place

CHAPTER 4

SUCCEEDING THROUGH PAIN

Just like diamonds are revealed from extreme pressure, the human spirit takes flight during adversity. I will go as far as to say we don't know what we're fully made of until we've experienced our absolute bottom. I can't predict what pain will cause you to do any more than you can foretell how my tragedies will affect me. But having lived through them is a testimony of what we can endure. Don't deny what you've overcome. Instead, use every memory of it to help you climb. Being lied on or mistreated are definitely situations we don't want to experience regularly, but there is a freedom in knowing how to live well on the other side of it. Living well means without animosity, spite, and bitterness. But with hope, joyful anticipation, and forgiveness. Suffering loss means you're human. None of us can engage consistently in life and never experience loss. Having experienced loss is not the same as "losing". Losing is a state of mind, whereas loss is collateral damage from living. There's no way to win at life if you choose to stop living!

Your perspective is valuable and should never be ignored, although only the accurate perspective is true reality. So many things influence perspective until it's often difficult to determine the truth. If I perceive someone as dishonest, trust may or may not be within reach. Perception occupies more mass than evidence. Recently, I watched a crime documentary about a very horrific murder. Two small children were at home with their mom. While the dad was away, the wife was violently beaten, dragged throughout the residence, and bludgeoned to death on the kitchen floor. The next day, as the six-year-old daughter was being questioned, she told authorities she saw everything. She said, "He had on a mask, and his eyes looked like my daddy's eyes, but it couldn't have been my daddy, because who would take care of me and my baby brother?" Reestablishing what or how someone believes is extremely difficult - even when they witness the proof with their own eyes.

Sometimes we're made to feel like we don't have worthy contributions. To dismiss your voice, is to label your experiences, relationships, and interactions as worthless. We all have a responsibility to present our lives as "meaningful". We do that by allowing the totality of everything that helped or hindered us to speak up. Put in the work to analyze the 'why' - but even when the answers are elusive, your insight on certain subjects is extremely valuable. Seasons that feel dormant are not uncommon, but we are thriving even when it doesn't look like it. When a broken foot is placed in a hard cast for six weeks, you don't notice the healing that's taking place. You can't see it or feel it, but the necessary movement

Seated in Your Rightful Place

is occurring every single day. Don't allow anyone to talk you down from your message. Remember that; even as you strive to attain the most accurate perspective. The puzzle pieces of your life connect the way they do for a reason. Please don't muffle that broadcast.

Behaviors change, but unfortunately most people never really do. Our beliefs and even our actions are shaped by the institutions that foster us. Rather than expelling so much energy trying to convince others they should be different, wake up to the biases that are inherent within yourself. None of us are without room for renovation. When you meet someone and they tell you who they are, believe them. Your mission in life should be to improve yourself- not to change others. The caveat is, when people are impressed by the way you live, they develop a watchful eye to adopt your strategies. Winning at being you involves winning people, not necessarily changing them.

Seated in Your Rightful Place

When we seek to change people, it suggests that we don't accept who they are. No one is who they were yesterday. And hopefully we'll be a better version tomorrow. The more I engage in the world, the more enlightened I become.

It's through that empowerment that tolerance is nurtured. But tolerance isn't enough. I can never say that I am complete until I genuinely love all. I (like you) am still in the fight to love all.

It's difficult to give people opportunities you never received. It's next to natural to want that for our own offspring, but to desire favor for others, goes beyond what's typical. Using your platform to assist others doesn't become an option until you're no longer carrying animosity some people never overcome. If you've watched hospital dramas, you've witnessed scenes that depict someone dying and a family having only minutes to decide whether or not to allow the donation of their family member's organs. A couple's child has just been pronounced brain-dead, and they're being told

Seated in Your Rightful Place

that a patient across the hall will die if they don't receive that heart. Imagine the range of emotions they're forced to process. In the end, they decide that it would be selfish to stand by and allow that patient to die - and they sign the consent form to donate the heart. That makes for a great television moment, but how many of us are truly living to give the advantage to someone else? I'm not suggesting that it makes you a bad person for choosing differently. Simply considering whether to step up to help someone else is more than what some people are willing to do.

Seated in Your Rightful Place

CHAPTER 5

LEARNING TO FORGIVE

When you think of all the things that haven't gone right in your life, do you envision certain people? As you're scrolling through social media and see specific names, what types of emotions do you experience? Make sure you don't have too many people surrounding your heart. Some people we hold onto are not even connected to us, and we must let them go. Use what they did to you as fuel, but separate the action from the person. Forgiveness is a sign of growth. It's not only something you give to others - you give it to yourself. When we release people, we make room for others. We let go of thoughts that clutter our creative flow, and embrace the freedom forgiveness affords. Some people we're at odds with hurt us unintentionally. Not all of our wounds are without our involvement. Sometimes we play just as much a role in what went bad as the person we characterize as the villain. I'm just saying take a closer look, and be fair, just, and true to yourself. Extending forgiveness doesn't mean the person goes free - but you become free of whatever barrier has stifled your productivity.

Some of us are carrying wounds inflicted by family members. These are some of the hardest to overcome, as we should be safest amongst people in our bloodline. If anyone has my back, shouldn't it be a family member? These betrayals cut so deep because they're unexpected. You typically don't plan for it, and almost no explanation makes sense. Many people have become authors because of the therapeutic benefits of writing out their story. Sometimes transferring the pain to a manuscript helps people process what they've come through. Confronting people face-to- face about harm they've caused isn't always easy to do. It's sometimes easier to talk about it with someone who has no affiliation with what occurred. Do whatever it takes to find the healthiest way for you to begin your healing journey.

Forgive yourself for time you've wasted. We are all guilty of that. Depending on how many things you've juggled simultaneously, you may have been unaware of your poor time management. Nevertheless, spent time is something that can never be redeemed. Memorializing lost time is a trivial pursuit, so I say, let's put all of our energy into what it takes to go forward.

We may never understand why people have acted callously toward us. Once you have earnestly checked your involvement, you must shake as much of that old residue as you can off your feet and keep it moving. Remaining in dark places too long perpetuates sabotaging behaviors. Winning at being you always requires a clear focus.

Seated in Your Rightful Place

Stop ignoring your compliments. Take inventory of them all. People tend to comment about things they don't see all the time. Even when we don't think there's anything special about the way we do things, I guarantee you no one can beat you at being you. Some things agitate us because we're on assignment to change them. Missionaries, James and Betty Robison, cannot solve the world's problem of hunger and thirst on their own, but what a glaring spotlight they've placed on the issue. They've been compelled for many years to work on it, affect it, sacrifice for it - because of their heart for people. If you're having trouble honing in on your special attributes, begin paying more attention to what others say about you. Be careful here. We've already discussed how it's not 'ultimately' about what people think of you. But establishing a reputation for specific traits is something that warrants your attention. If you choose to step up to be the solution to some of the problems you notice in the world – and begin transferring those agitating feelings into positive action, you'll move yet closer to discovering what really has meaning for you. Attracting people to partner with you to solve global problems like hunger and thirst, won't be accomplished with rhetoric that's cruel and divisive. Love and kindness is what draws people. Even if James and Betty Robison believed a certain population of people are responsible for hunger and thirst, unforgiveness wouldn't strengthen their mission. Forgiveness takes faith. When you give it, you're believing for continued freedom to live with clarity of mind and hope. However, faithless people become unforgiving people, and unforgiveness rots the soul.

Seated in Your Rightful Place

CHAPTER 6

EXPERIENCE TOTAL FREEDOM

Unless you learn to love yourself, you can never comprehend the merit of walking in your freedom. In fact, you can't identify freedom if you don't realize you're bound. Knowing you're enchained sets you on a course to discover your liberty. Bondage isn't always overt - it can be very subtle. However, you'll never know how restricted you are if you never experience total freedom. What do you mean when you say total freedom? I'm living better than I ever have. I've become more than my parents ever imagined. What about what you've imagined for yourself? Now that you've wrapped yourself as a pretty gift under the tree for your parents, the next chapter belongs to you. There is a freedom of mind, body, and soul waiting for you, but it will not fall into your lap. With the freedom of being comes the freedom of doing. A total mindset change occurs because the light is now turned on. You are literally in the dark when you're bound. The light of freedom illuminates pathways you could never see before. Come out of the shadows and start making things happen. Put on your confidence that the key ingredient the world's been missing, is you. You've fulfilled the waiting period. The time has finally come for you to demonstrate who you are. Don't violate principles - just work them like a boss. It's not about changing who you are, but infusing yourself into what's going on around you. In some instances, you don't make the difference, you ARE the difference! If you never learn that about yourself, not only will you be cheated, but the world will be penalized. Perhaps you have the cure for the disease in my body, the song that can soothe the rage within, the book that will

Seated in Your Rightful Place

inspire millions to thrive, or the invention that will bring ease to the most tedious task. Only you know, or do you?

Aren't you tired of being stumped by questions you've never pondered? It's time to switch things up. Begin asking yourself the tough questions, because you'll be asked one way or another. Will it be now - when you can make adjustments and implement strategies for successful intervention? Or will you continue the cycle of waiting; to the detriment of having no time left to respond? What is the prize I take home for learning my true self? Knowing who you are gives you permission to say yes to the things you should do, and no to the things you shouldn't. Yes it's really that simple - and it's not an understatement. If you can ever learn to love yourself more, the internal battles that often plague you will begin to dissipate.

Do-overs are amazing! We don't always have to look to re-create ourselves - just pay attention to what's in front of you. Life sometimes gives us second chances. Initially we

39

Seated in Your Rightful Place

are hurt when we're shut out of planning we weren't part of. The decision to pull you off a project, your transfer to another city, or totally phasing out your job are events that can uproot anyone's life. We may lay down as victims for a brief moment, so long as we get back on our feet with a plan. If you've not yet experienced such a pivotal moment, it's coming. Are you prepared for it? Having financial assurances in place is definitely a big factor, but as an earner going forward, have you begun strategizing for a life of joy, peace, and invigoration? These are not the times of old, when everyone in your community had to work at the factory. Expand your community mentally and physically. Today, wealth is born from creative ideas. Don't you want some of that?

Have you noticed the type of people you attract? Is there a common theme for how people become close to you? Better yet, are there people you actually repel? Recently I discovered that although I have many acquaintances, I don't have a large number of very close friends. Of course the definition of a "very close friend" is relative from person to person - but I find myself desiring to be a better friend.

I was raised in Kansas, and in high school I attended Washington High for 9th and 10th grade. I had what I considered to be great relationships. At the beginning of year 3, because of zoning, I was required to attend F.L. Schlagle High for both 11th and 12th grade. I was about as resilient as any kid could be in that type of situation. But I felt I had to trade the bonds I formed at Washington for my new relationships at Schlagle. At that time, none of it really mattered much. But several years later I began questioning the depth of my relationships. I've never been adopted, but the only thing that comes close to what I can compare it to is the feeling of being ripped away from one family and placed in another. What's the significance? Unless you put out an APB for answers, there will forever be questions. The questions I have may not matter much to you, but we're different people with different missions. When you find yourself reflecting, and happen upon memories that seem suspect, do you investigate? The mind is tricky. You can retell your life's history multiple times without realizing you're omitting key elements. Our brain has the potential to rewrite scripts in an attempt to protect us from facing what actually transpired. Have you ever noticed old friends having a totally different account of your story? My intention is not to draw you into therapy, but to impress upon you the significance of knowing the factual details of your past.

Somehow winning always presupposes there must be a loser. I don't want to imply that you can live your entire life and end it with the label of "loser". I believe this manuscript is packed with jewels for helping you max out living your best life. But let's be clear, not heeding my advice does not a loser make. What's so awesome about this life God has given us, is that there are several roads to get us to the path we should ultimately be on. Even now (while authoring this book) I'm embarrassed by how many times I ignored mistakes I knew I was actively making. The most important part of every journey is reaching your destination. If the navigation systems in our vehicles stopped offering routes just because we keep making wrong turns, we'd get rid of them. We've grown accustomed to knowing there's always another way. Yes, I'm so thankful that grace is a very real thing. But I also caution anyone who is of the belief that grace for every situation never runs out.

Seated in Your Rightful Place

CHAPTER 7

THE HIGH COST OF LOW LIVING

There is an extremely high cost for low living. Let's talk about low living. This has nothing to do with socio-economic status, but everything to do with daily output. Things that require small amounts of energy, and take almost no time to finish are referred to as "low hanging fruit". Tasks that demand more than an hour of focus, and a sustained amount of energy are sometimes called "high hanging fruit". While easy things are often considered to be lazy things to do, they are sometimes the best solutions for complex problems. Many times we overthink opportunities that are right in front of us. Even if your goal is to do bigger and better things, there's nothing wrong with choosing low hanging fruit when it presents itself. I'm a list maker, which means I evaluate my daily success by how many tasks I'm able to mark as "done". There have always been people who've told me I shouldn't be this way, and that I should change my outlook to guard myself from disappointment. Instead, I began to see this attribute as an asset. Conquering small, trivial tasks early in the day sykes me up and mentally prepares me to begin confronting the high hanging fruit.

Let's take a look at the flipside. What if no individual or situation ever places the right amount of pressure on us? Get to a mirror and look inside. Ask yourself, "Have I somehow mastered looking the other way, stifling my own growth and creativity"? An empowerment strategy I often employ when equipping background singers is to challenge them to learn everyone's part. In other words, if you're singing alto, learn the tenor and soprano parts as well. The primary reason is navigational - knowing where others are, helps you monitor where you should be. The other reason for this strategy is to be a team player. If you train your ear to hear what's missing, you can instantaneously sing that part (providing the solution). I once had someone respond by saying, "I'm only here to sing my part". I caution you to not be the person who won't at least try for more. I wouldn't use the word impossible, but I think it is very unlikely to rise to our highest heights without sponsors - people who will push or pull us beyond what's comfortable. It may even be beneficial to tag in different people for the different areas of your life.

An unguarded strength is a double weakness. There's not much worse than being talked out of a necessary skill you already master. When you don't know the complete value of what you possess, you invest very little to protect it. Don't forget how to take chances on yourself. For so long, many of us have tried to convince others that we are worth the risk. We've been trying to market ourselves tirelessly, but do we really believe in the product? Do we think we're ready for

Seated in Your Rightful Place

a record label to invest in us, or spectacular enough for a company to offer us an endorsement deal? Fainting starts in the mind. If you don't believe you're capable, it will always be difficult to convince anyone otherwise.

Here's the thing, not many people at this juncture ever feel ready - but it's the belief they have in themselves that overpowers the insecurities. The biggest and greatest risk one could ever take, is to bet on yourself. Betting on yourself is not the same as choosing one perspective over another. Betting on yourself means to begin trusting your tendencies - your gut belief. The decisions you sometimes have to make when betting on yourself seem risky, but that may be due to you being outside of your comfort zone. There's no fallback guy when betting on yourself. You are the blame, but you'll have to start getting comfortable with shouldering the burden. As a worship leader/ choir director, I tell people all the time during rehearsals that mistakes should be made out loud. That gives us an opportunity to know something's wrong and needs tweaking. Don't be silently wrong during the dress rehearsal, and super loud during the performance. That's backwards. Finding out that you're making mistakes is always an uncomfortable feeling, but would you rather know and change, or sink because of ignorance? It's hard to trust yourself when you don't have a winning record. But if anyone is worth the risk, shouldn't it be you?

Just because something didn't work before, doesn't automatically mean it won't work now. Persistence definitely has its place. There are seasons for everything in life, and sometimes we're simply trying to operate in the wrong season. Running a successful business, or thriving in any large venture requires many things working in sync. If you've tried to launch your rocket and the mission failed, reschedule a lift-off. NASA does it all the time. Years of man hours and millions of dollars are invested in building space shuttles and rockets. Many things can deter a mission's

Seated in Your Rightful Place

outcome - bad weather, mechanical failures, etc. Even when you've accounted for the worst possible occurrences, your contingency plans may not be enough. But if you know without question that you're in the right fight, fight on! By the end, it may not look as it did at its conception, but that's still a victory. Change is good but be careful of compromise. Whenever compromise is involved, someone is always trying to get you to move your line. Imagine a scenario where you've invented a wonder drug you anxiously want to make available to the public.

Compromising your timeframe to wait another year could result in millions of lives lost. Just how valuable is your cargo, and how much are you willing to lose by not walking in your privilege?

CHAPTER 8

EXPECTATION IS CONNECTED TO DECLARATION

Can you imagine a life different from the one you're living? Most people can't. Sure, we're good at the what-if game (What if I won the lottery? What if I inherited a fortune?). But can you truly make a distinction in your imagination between fictional thinking and reality thinking? Some thoughts are only to soothe and pacify, while others are meant to shake the foundation of your life. There's a difference between talking about something and declaring it to be so. I need what I'm striving for to be more than just an illusion. Real change always begins as a captivating thought, but if your dreams will ever sprout legs and begin to walk in the physical realm, it will be largely due to what's coming out of your mouth. Whether it's obtaining wealth, or simply being emotionally consistent, we must pull it into our lives so it becomes part of us. As long as I have no requirement to work any strategies to retain it, it is but a fleeting thought. As often as you can, begin voicing your intentions for the future. Our words add pressure, and they box us in. Being boxed in isn't always a bad thing. It forces us to make good on our commitments - or at least face the music.

Don't be more honored by the position than obligated by your purpose. The truth is, we're not qualified for every job we apply for. But sometimes it's awarded to us - knowing we're not suited for it at all. Being extremely impressive, and possessing attributes that draw people in are admirable talents. When talent is used disingenuously to mislead, it's very manipulative. Sure, in the beginning it's easy to see how you may have manipulated others, but perhaps not so apparent that you've deceived yourself. Contentment comes from fulfilling purpose. Obviously there's nothing wrong with commanding a huge salary, a corner office, and the other amenities associated with acquiring a great position - but does the work you do sustain your peace of mind? Growing beyond a paycheck is very difficult to do, and I am totally aware that many people never arrive at comprehending such a thing. As you age and start questioning certain voids, sometimes you discover that the problem with your output has everything to do with your employment.

How we serve others determines how effective we'll be as leaders. Good leadership requires an ability to have and understand empathy. You don't always have to have walked someone's full journey to be able to relate to them. You must; however, have the social capacity to build bridges that allow you to connect. It's natural to erect barriers when forming new relationships. If someone shared everything about

Seated in Your Rightful Place

themselves during your first encounter, you'd think that was weird. There are people with disarming personalities who cause us to share more than we normally would, but usually not everything immediately. I must earn the right to know your story, and unless you trust me, you won't be sharing matters of the heart. If perhaps you're not yet the boss, take advantage of being in the interim by cultivating your work relationships. Learn everything you can from your employer - what works and what doesn't work. You can never ascend higher than the level of your associations.

Dare to be an exhibitionist. Of course I'm not being vulgar, but once you cast inhibitions to the wind, new pathways appear. Some personalities are wrapped so tight, that personal desire has never been on the table for consideration. Our upbringing (station, formula) for "how things are done" kicks in. Seldom do people try different alternatives for living. Think about it as it relates to food and culture. Certain meals have become staples in our homes - not just because of how they taste, but because they've become part of our traditions. For some of us, specific holidays require specific dishes. We won't even entertain switching it up. There's comfort with the normalcy of it. If only It was as simple as just being a food trap. No way my friend. Usually where there's one trap, there are likely many more. By definition, an exhibitionist bares all. Nothing is hidden because all is revealed. It's much easier to let go of inhibitions when you're literally naked. Purpose to shed more, so you can actually see what's hanging and needs to come off. Trimming the excess from your life is one of the most difficult tasks there are. Even when we want to do it, and see that it's necessary, we can't always do what needs to be done. Disciplining our flesh is such a challenge. Even when we can successfully say no to others, we can't always deny ourselves things we know are causing us harm. Utilize effective strategies. Decide ahead of time what you will and will not do, and make it known to your accountability partners. Giving them permission to coach you makes you less vulnerable to

Seated in Your Rightful Place

failure. A team is mightier than an individual, so link arms with comrades. As long as the members of your team are aligned with a similar focus, you're better together. Strength is intensified once it becomes unified. Success in life should not only be about reaching our personal goals, but joining with others who are also in pursuit of an amazing life.

When I think of banding together for a common purpose, I think of the greatest wildlife spectacle on earth. Each year the Serengeti plains in Tanzania play host to one of the greatest animal migrations in the world. 2.5 million Mammals (including wildebeests and zebras) begin a round trip that will take them almost 2000 miles. What initiates the migration to begin is unknown, as there is no discernible signal, but when one goes, they all go. As they cross the treacherous Mara River, crocodiles, cheetah, and lions lie in wait. Despite great danger, the wildebeest herds always complete their migration. Are you willing to complete your journey at all costs?

CHAPTER 9

WHAT CAN YOU LIVE WITHOUT

If you get to where you're going, where will you be? If you accomplish your goals, what will you have? Everybody's not meant to be a celebrity, a multi-millionaire, an entrepreneur, etc. Some men will never be husbands. Some wives will never be mothers. Surely you see how broad this list can expand. I'm not mentioning these things so you'll feel better about what you've not been able to obtain. It's simply a fact that none of us can have everything we want - none of us! The things most people desire for their lives are normal, right, and good. Some desires are extravagant, while others are very basic, but that has no bearing on them being desires we can justify. There are many reasons why we want the things we do, and I'm certainly not going to challenge you to qualify your list of wants. I will however, challenge you to create a list of what you cannot live without. Seriously invest some time in this activity, because most of us are unaware of just how much we can live without. I must forewarn you that this activity tends to inspire more thought-provoking questions. Does not having the manifestation of your complete list of desires make you irrelevant, ineffective, without influence? If your outlook is negative, then your answer to this question is yes. Sometimes optimism affords us a perspective ignorance would never allow us to see.

Since no one can beat you at being you, and you can't adequately measure your growth against another's, how do you know when you're winning? When you're being inspired more than influenced, awakened more than drawn, focused more than intrigued, and content more than satisfied, you are winning. Winning as your best self requires you to stop apologizing for decisions that may seem unconventional. Don't cast traditional wisdom into the trash bin, just use it as a starting point. You are winning when you're winning in health, joy, peace, fulfillment, and purpose. That's true prosperity! You are not in the final testament of your life. Today's pages that describe you fall short of defining you. The half has not been told, or why even deal with this subject matter? My failed marriage, moderate health, and slight bank account are not the testimony I want for my life, but life is still in process. God, the ultimate coach, has a playbook that will cause our despair to experience a transforming tilt. Things don't even begin to change until you expect to see different results. Stop accepting what's always been as what you'll always have. That doesn't have to be your story.

What if your time and energy have been spent, and you're just coming into the awareness of the alternative you? As humans, we are multi-faceted. We have the ability to maneuver, shift, and bend to meet our challenges. There

Seated in Your Rightful Place

will forever be legitimate reasons why we can't be winners. After you leave the pity party, begin to develop an outside game. Michael Jordan is revered as one of the greatest to have ever played the game of basketball. When he entered the NBA, he was extremely agile and his ability to take the ball directly to the basket was almost never impaired. As defenses were mounted to be more physical, Michael began to pay the price through injuries. Because of injuries, age, and fatigue (legitimate reasons for a loss in productivity) Michael extended his game to include other threats. Opponents had learned how to defend his inside game, but he developed an offensive repertoire of threats just as potent from the outside. Use the energy, platform, and tools you have to do what you can now. There's nothing we can do about what didn't happen except use the experience of the wait to intensify your passion.

Relax and enjoy the really good days, because they're not all full of clouds. There are moments when we must let our guard down. I'm not saying you should open yourself up to be preyed upon, but sometimes when our defenses are too tight - we lose proper perspective. We work so hard to control the comings and goings of our life at the expense of missing the beauty of each day's natural flow. In sports they say, "Let the game come to you", which simply means - before you try to make something happen, take a look at what's presented. One man's turnover becomes extra points for his opponent. Things are only stress-worthy when you set them up to be that way. As a child, I grew up not knowing we were broke. We were prosperous with love, church and community connectivity, faith, and hope - but eight people sharing one bathroom and three bedrooms is "broke". My mom and dad never let on that we were in lack. The 'joy barometer' in our 1000 square-foot house was always on

Seated in Your Rightful Place

high. I'm not saying my dad didn't worry. I'm saying if he was worried, I never smelled it on him, so I dreamed (as kids should) rather than wasting time worrying. What's the aroma like in your house? Are you perpetuating debilitating jargon that might keep your kids in mental bondage for years to come? It's no secret that our kids repeat what we say, but let your actions be more worthy of imitating.

It's easy to be knocked off balance when responding to things based on a first glance. A glance is not an actual picture, but a fragment of perception. It's enough to draw us in, but too unreliable to build upon. It is however, a necessary spark to cause an interruption in our thinking. Think of a glance as a glimmer of "what if". What if I start my own company? What if I apply myself and become certified in this other area? What if I go back to school to pursue a master's degree? All are examples of what could be, but not really actionable without real purpose. Sure, anything positive is worth starting, but the test is to follow through to completion. If we've not resolved that our glance is more than just a good idea, there's no way to mount the intensity required to go all the way. Don't choose the paths of others just because. It's alright if you stumble into knowing your purpose; just don't let who you become be an accident.

Seated in Your Rightful Place

CHAPTER 10

DON'T FALL INTO THE TRAP

Minimizing the importance of discovering your true potential is a trap most people fall victim of. It was through the eyes of my youngest brother, Christopher, that I began paying attention to my ability to write as a gift. For whatever reason, it happens that way sometimes. We don't place a lot of value on the things we haven't worked to earn. But just because we're naturally good at something, doesn't mean it mustn't be developed and sharpened. A mistake we make is thinking that everybody is just as good at the skill as we are. Instead of celebrating our gifts, we sometimes hide them. Some love the ability they have, but not the attention it brings. What a frustrating position to be in. If you are relating to this, you're not the first. There are many documented testimonials by people who fought to overcome debilitating situations in order to give rise to their true talents.

Steve Harvey overcame a stuttering problem to realize his dream of becoming a television and radio personality. Charlotte Brown defied blindness to be a successful pole-vaulter. Robert Downey Jr. denounced drug addiction to become one of Hollywood's top earners. Emma Stone overcame shyness and panic attacks in her pursuit to become one of Hollywood's actress sweethearts. At the age of 14, Oprah Winfrey survived rape and the loss of a child – and used the tragedies as fuel to become a broadcast mogul. You must find a way over, around, or through your obstacles for winning. Your purpose depends upon it.

Would the life you're chasing continue to be the life you're chasing if you remained anonymous after getting the prize?

Are you seeking a level of prestige to prove a point or make your name great? No judgment here. It takes all types of motivation to get us from where we are to where we hope to be. The important thing is to know what's fueling your fight. Some young fathers have only been able to remain constant in the home because of a promise they made themselves long ago to be better than their father, and not leave. Some women never accept a proposal for marriage due to a vow they made to never be smothered like their mom in a marriage with a chauvinistic partner. Concessions will always be made along the way for what we are aspiring to, just make sure it's something you're giving and not something you're giving up. Think about this. If when you donate, you never do it anonymously - explore why that is. For some, the simple act of releasing something of need into a circumstance that will empower someone else is all the reward they need. Others require you to know they gave it, and expect you to formally thank them, including a status report of how the donation was used. Again, this is just an

Seated in Your Rightful Place

observation without judgment. What a shame it would be to amass every tangible desire on your list and still lack the feeling of wholeness.

Something we all have in common is that none of us have lived our best moments every day. Despite your religion, your belief in God, fate, or karma, it's impossible for everyday to be prolific. I've heard people say, "I don't have bad days", and I get it. Your outlook is the filter for the moments you experience. If honesty is at play, even the most optimistic people will admit that some days totally out-rank others. Not that I give up on the day, but sometimes by 11 am I can already tell, "today is one of those days". It's when you feel you're forcing a 75-pound square ball to roll up hill.

When you're experiencing these types of days, it's important to allow yourself some grace for tomorrow. Regrouping and strategizing for tomorrow is sometimes the best plan for today.

In 2014, Tom Cruise starred in a movie called "Edge Of Tomorrow". He was a soldier who died in battle, but once he died, his life would reset to the same moment. He could prolong his life using the strategies and information he'd acquired in his former life, but ultimately, he could never trick death. I know that's make-believe, but similarly I've taught my brain to quickly recognize when a "mental health day" is underway. Stay in position to be strong for tomorrow rather than unnecessarily burning out due to depletion.

Stand on the shoulders of all those who tossed their excuses aside and dared to be great - not to be admired, but to be true to themselves. Every life journey is for the benefit of all. We may feel that we're living in isolation at times, but what you do in your lifetime ultimately speaks out loud. Recognize and combat your fears with the power of intention. You're only a victim if it's a label you choose. Those we revere as great haven't always thought that of themselves. Some would even disagree with the depiction. But they stand out to us

Seated in Your Rightful Place

because where they ended up is miles and miles away from where they began. Although their story cannot be yours, use the mountains they've climbed to motivate you until you've scaled your own.

It's not always our decision when our roles change in people's lives. When we're celebrated and asked for more, it feels really good, but when people transition away from us, a series of things begin to happen. There's no specific list and order because it's based on our experience and personality. Usually when people walk away, the most recognized comment is, "It's not personal". Whether it's a business or romantic relationship, all separations on some level are personal. Who we are to people shifts, and our influence with them can go from hero to zero. Don't let it cripple you, but allow yourself to feel everything associated with the shift. Take what was good about the process and incorporate that in your relationships going forward. Retool what was done badly towards you so when you initiate transitions in roles in the future, you are more relational. There's no substitution for respect!

What about people who seem happiest when bringing misfortune to others? Are they winning at being who they are? Obviously, mental health plays a significant role in all of our lives. There are some on the extreme side who engage in behavior such as murder and rape - confusing the exchange with gratification. And we all know some people on the lower end of the spectrum who would never physically harm anyone, but seemingly make it a daily practice to cause you hell. Are these people who are inflicting dread living their best life? I'm no psycho analyst or psychiatrist, but the short answer is "no". It is my desire that this manuscript will provoke all of us who feel we've done due diligence in analyzing who we are, how we got here, and what we want in life to continue the scrutiny.

Seated in Your Rightful Place

CHAPTER 11

YOUR TESTIMONY IS
YOUR RESUME

What you become known for may actually subsidize the purpose you are intended to champion. It happens more often than you may think; multi-millionaires totally unfulfilled, on a quest to do something altogether different. Some athletes retire from their sport (while still in their prime) to reinvent themselves in business. Successful business owners sell their companies to pursue more invigorating challenges. Perhaps an invention, a heroic act, or a rare talent ushered you onto the world's stage. Being able to parlay that into a residual earning stream is admirable, but is that alone enough to fulfill your life? Winning at being you is more than being financially rich, but wealthy in mind, body, and soul. Arriving at millionaire status prior to finding one's true self is definitely 'a thing'. Since the majority of people can't relate to the notion, this small community gets labels when they go against the grain - like capricious and petulant. They are ignored because people who have no money problems have no real problems. Right? Of course that's not right. The foundation of happiness begins with choosing to be happy. On the surface it would seem that someone with lots of money could easily choose to compare their life to someone who doesn't have money - and that itself should ignite happiness. It's a flame only created by just the right spark. The spark that sets off my explosion of happiness changes with each year of my journey. If this were not true, why is the rate of divorce more than 50%? Why is domestic abuse amongst intimate partners who chose each other so prevalent? Finding the flame to ignite our happiness isn't always fleeting, but understand that the pursuit is lifelong.

I'm having trouble writing this book without including some of my personal experiences. I do it because it helps me to be accountable with the truth. Why put words on a page that don't reveal as much as they possibly can? Most adults have (at minimum) six jobs they are responsible for doing simultaneously. For instance, one woman reading this book's jobs might be wife, mother, school teacher, church choir director, math tutor, and cheerleading sponsor. Each of these roles carries enormous responsibilities, and not being at your best affects many lives. Even when we change jobs, it's difficult to release roles we are no longer responsible for.

Some roles we accept as being lifelong, and treat them as such. There is a part of my brain that still hasn't resolved that my 29 year marriage is no longer. After eight years of being without a mate, I still wrestle with not feeling guilty for planning and doing things just for my own personal enjoyment. Not that it was a chore to always consider

Seated in Your Rightful Place

my spouse when we were married; it's just that it's very different now.

The only One who's original intent becomes actual reality is God. True progress is more about being on the right path than having things line up the way we expect. Over time I've learned how to make my prayers less like I'm praying to a genie granting wishes. We tend to ask for what we want, but with limited knowledge and in most cases, zero wisdom. I now realize that it's God who removes the blinders and enables me to see more and more. He's actually been waiting for me to connect my train car to Him, rather than attempting to be the engine. I have no clue sometimes how I end up in a position of blessings, but God is never caught off guard. We manipulate people so badly sometimes, trying to make our agenda fit into their's. Connections are often simple interventions to pull you from one path to another. Don't force it to be more. When you pray, ask God for wisdom, not people.

As I'm overcoming, the more fit I become. The more I personally witness myself accomplish, the more my brain accepts that it's possible. The moves I make contribute to my resume because it shows I'm not done. It's a testimonial for my own encouragement. I hit walls at times that tell me I've gone as far as I can go. If progress has no limit (which it doesn't) then I must feed from a source that's cheering me forward. No matter how small, my own story from yesterday is the best indicator of what's behind the curtain of accomplishment for me today. You will always be able to find someone who has a larger net worth than you, a better physique, a more appealing voice, etc. Those comparisons can't be the measure for whether or not you're winning. Sure, it feels good to impress others - but it feels great when we realize we can still impress ourselves. Have you impressed yourself lately? What action would it take to cause you to pound your chest in celebration of you? You'd be surprised how something seemingly minuscule can change the trajectory of an entire day. What's most exhilarating

Seated in Your Rightful Place

about progress is its range of motion. We typically try to measure progress vertically; however, vertical growth leaves us with such a limited and misleading characterization. If the starting point guard on my basketball team, averaging 40 points per game, suddenly experienced a 50% drop in points scored - how would you rate him? This same player has doubled his assists, increased his rebounds and steals, and improved his free- throw shooting percentage. If you only focus on points per game, you'd say this player has declined - but if you focus on the overall stats, it's obvious much growth has occurred. The key is learning to focus on the positives.

A FINAL THOUGHT

Nothing ever really happens by chance. Whether this book was given to you as a gift, or you happened to find it on your own, it was an appointment you were destined to have. Think of it as a crossroads. I believe God loves us so much that He gives us opportunities for enhancements. He sees us desiring improvement for our lives, and He plants seeds for the manifestation to occur. Let's call your reading this book an interruption, a slap in the face, a car accident - something unexpected to jolt you into a new mindset. I am definitely a science-fiction movie lover. I love futuristic movies like "The Terminator". As the characters leap through time continuums, people can't fathom what's really going on because they have an inability to relate. The information they're being asked to quickly process is literally from another world. Guard this book as such. The life within you to live and the life you're currently living are worlds apart.

Seated in Your Rightful Place

You're not just "not winning", you're "not living". As I've said, God would not reveal things to you about yourself and not give you a way of escape - so escape from your dungeons of doom to enlightenment and expression!

Seated in Your Rightful Place

Throne Proclamations

👑 Strength is intensified once it becomes unified.

👑 Sometimes optimism affords us a perspective ignorance would never allow us to see.

👑 Some love the ability they have, but not the attention it brings.

👑 Concessions will always be made along the way for what we are aspiring to, just make sure it's something you're giving and not something you're giving up

👑 Regrouping and strategizing for tomorrow is sometimes the best plan for today.

👑 It's not fair, but we're responsible for what we don't know.

👑 Just as critical as the butterfly making its own metamorphosis from the cocoon, or the baby chick pecking for freedom from the eggshell - pushing through barriers is what qualifies us mentally to withstand physically.

👑 A goal-oriented person should not require an external stimulus in order to be productive.

👑 Your ability to internalize information is greatly determined by your connection to it.

👑 The very concerns you disregard along the way, will confront you at the most inopportune times.

👑 There's a difference between talking about something and declaring it to be so.

Seated in Your Rightful Place

ABOUT THE AUTHOR

DR. JOHN DAVID MCCONNELL

Dr. John David McConnell is the owner of Prolyric Productions Publishing Company. Born and raised in Kansas City Kansas, John received his Bachelor of Science degree at Saint Mary College in Leavenworth, Kansas. John taught grades 2 through 8 over the span of his 27-year career as a public-school educator. 20 of those years were with the Houston Independent School District.

In 2016 John received his doctorate in sacred music from Christian Bible Institute & Seminary. His war chest of badges includes Christian, father of two sons, educator, actor, singer, songwriter, worship-leader, Certified Christian Counselor, and author. John exited his teaching career in 2022, and is currently pursuing his literary and songwriting careers full-time.

To Contact John McConnell:

johndmac4@aol.com

832-865-0260

Photography by: Stanton Trueheart

Seated in Your Rightful Place

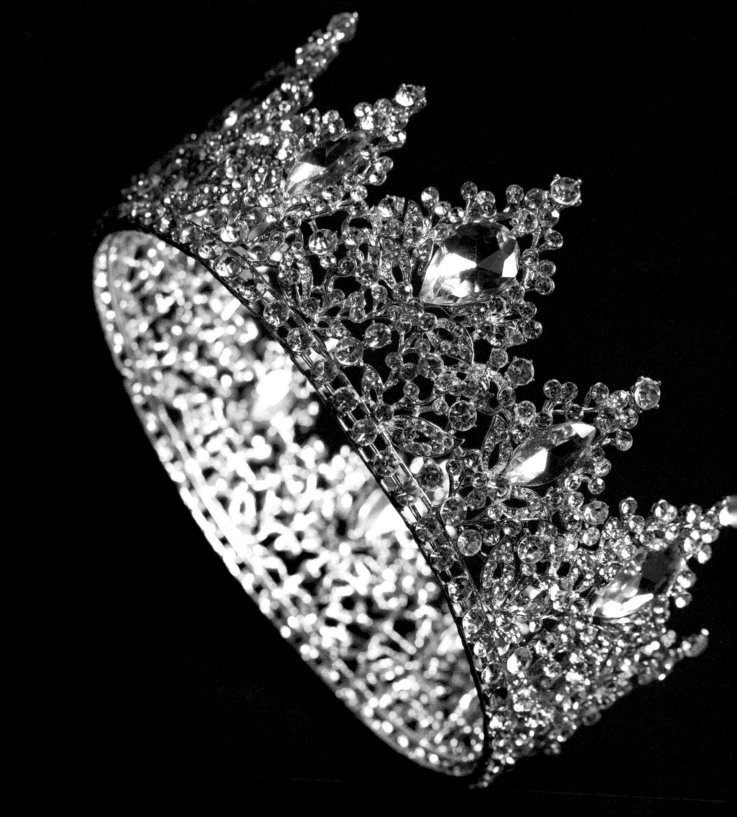

AMAZING PET STORIES 2

Written by: Carol B. Pangalos

Editor: Theresa Taliercio

Illustrator: Salvador Capuyan

Other Books Written by Carol B. Pangalos

Amazing Pet Stories

My Name is Skye

Where is Pinky's Mommy? (A Sequel to Gabriella and the Magic Stars)

Gabriella and the Magic Stars

Love, Patience and Understanding, Words from the Heart

Yvonne and Carol - Bloodsisters Forever

AuthorHouse™
1663 Liberty Drive
Bloomington, IN 47403
www.authorhouse.com
Phone: 833-262-8899

This book is printed on acid-free paper.

ISBN: 979-8-8230-2498-3 (sc)
ISBN: 979-8-8230-2499-0 (e)
ISBN: 979-8-8230-2666-6 (hc)

Print information available on the last page.

Published by AuthorHouse 05/17/2024

authorHOUSE®

Dedicated to My Three Grandchildren

Gabriella

Luke Michael

Skye Khloe

And

My Husband, Michael G. Pangalos

THE MOUSE IN THE HOUSE

This is a true story about a little mouse who became friends with an elderly lady named Agnes. Everyone called her Grandma Ma. She was 90 years old and lived alone. Although she lived alone, she was never lonely.

Her two grown children Eddie and Carol lived nearby.

Grandma Ma loved to cook and always kept a tidy, clean home. Eddie and Carol would take turns visiting her each day. They checked to see if she was well and if groceries were needed.

One sunny morning, Grandma Ma was washing dishes after eating breakfast. SUDDENLY, there was a little mouse staring at her! At first, she was frightened! She jumped back and yelled, "Go away, get off my kitchen counter and go back where you came from." The mouse did not move! HE CONTINUED STARING AT HER.

Grandma Ma did not know what to do next!! She decided to throw warm water on the little mouse. She hoped he would get wet and run away. HE DID GET WET, but he did not run away. Instead, he began tapping his tiny feet in the puddle of water that was splashed on the counter. He started squeaking and twirling around and around. HE WAS DANCING AND HAVING FUN!

Grandma Ma was not sure if she should smile or be upset with this little mouse. What would you do?

Later that day, her son came to visit her. She told him there was a mouse in her house. Eddie searched all the cabinets and walls to see if there were any openings for a mouse to go through. THERE WERE NO OPEN SPACES ANYWHERE! So how did this mouse enter his mom's home? NO ONE KNEW!

During the winter months, the mouse continued to be on the kitchen counter whenever Grandma Ma washed dishes. He would squeak, tap his feet and continuously twirl around in the puddle of water. Grandma Ma said to the mouse, "I am going to name you Squeaky the Dancing Mouse." Each time she saw the mouse, he made her HAPPY and he BRIGHTENED her day.

One chilly evening Grandma Ma sat in her favorite chair ready to relax. She heard a faint squeak. When she looked down on the floor, she saw Squeaky. She asked. "Are you cold my little friend? Here is a blanket to keep you warm." Squeaky looked up at Grandma Ma and squeaked twice. He then snuggled in the toasty warm blanket and fell asleep for the night. Squeaky felt very loved and comfortable living in Grandma Ma's home.

The next day, when Carol came to check on her mom, the mouse joined them in the living room and started squeaking, tapping his feet and twirling. Carol said to her mom, "I never saw a mouse dance and twirl." Grandma Ma then said, "Squeaky is an exceptional mouse! He is my special little friend."

The long winter months were coming to an end and Springtime was approaching. With the warmer weather, Grandma Ma noticed Squeaky was visiting her less and less. She missed seeing him EVERY DAY.

One morning when Grandma Ma was washing dishes, she looked up and **there** he was! Squeaky was **staring** at her once again! She was delighted to see him. She said with tears in her eyes, "There you are Squeaky. Where have you been? I missed you, but I am so happy you came back to see me." She started petting the top of Squeaky's head with a Grandma's loving touch.

Squeaky looked at Grandma Ma and began squeaking, tapping his feet and twirling around and around in the puddle of water on the counter. Just then he stood on his hind legs and WAVED at Grandma Ma. She wondered WHY he was WAVING! Was he WAVING "HELLO" OR "GOODBYE?" She was very puzzled and did not know what to think!

That was an exhausting day for Grandma Ma. She decided to sit in her chair and rest. When she looked down on the blanket, Squeaky WAS NOT THERE! He was not snuggled in his blanket and there were no more squeaks coming from him. Her house was so quiet, one could hear a pin drop!!!

The next day, Grandma Ma did all her usual morning routines. She was hoping to see Squeaky, **BUT HE WAS NOT THERE!** She missed watching his dancing and hearing his squeaks. She wondered if that was a "**GOODBYE**" forever wave? What do you think?

Many weeks passed and Squeaky never returned. Grandma Ma was hoping Squeaky was not hurt or lost. Her family knew how sad she was. They told her one day Squeaky will **SURPRISE** you again with his visit. Maybe it will be soon. Hearing these words from her children, Grandma Ma felt **HAPPY** once again.

Did you ever see a mouse tap his feet, twirl and dance?

Would you smile or be upset if a mouse splashed water on your kitchen counter?

Do you think Squeaky will ever come back to see Grandma Ma?

THE END.

"Squeak, Squeak, Squeak." Squeaky the Dancing Mouse wants you to always be HAPPY, JUMP IN PUDDLES, TWIRL AND HAVE FUN.

LIA'S FISHING ADVENTURES

One Sunday morning, a couple, Ellyn and Ken, decided to visit a rescue shelter hoping to adopt a puppy. They adopted an adult cat eight years ago and named her Bella. She is a red tabby with large yellow eyes. Her fur is soft and feels like silk.

The shelter had many cages filled with animals needing a forever home. There were all breeds of dogs, cats, kittens and puppies. There were rabbits, lizards, turtles, snakes, and different types of birds. The shelter was crowded with many people wanting to adopt a special pet for their family.

After seeing many adorable puppies, Ellyn said, "I wish we could adopt each one." Ken looked at her with a smile.

They noticed a cage in the corner of the shelter. This cage had much younger and smaller puppies in it. Many of the puppies were sleeping and nestled together.

When standing and looking into the cage, a tiny black and tan puppy walked towards them. She had the cutest little face with big brown eyes. Her fur was short and fuzzy. "Woof, Woof" she barked in a whisper. "Woof-Woof."

Both Ellyn and Ken wondered what this tiny puppy was trying to say to them. Perhaps she was asking, "Can you please take me home? Can you please choose me? If you do, I will love you forever."

Do you think this puppy wanted Ken and Ellyn to adopt her?

When Ellyn looked into the puppy's eyes, she instantly FELL IN LOVE. She knew at that moment this puppy was for them!

After the paperwork was completed, the puppy was handed to Ellyn. Ken and Ellyn were gleaming with joy. They were told their new puppy was 3 months old. She was a mixed terrier and she loved to snuggle.

Ellyn said, "Let's name her LIA. A beautiful name for our new puppy." Ken agreed! Now that Lia was theirs, they could not wait to bring her home. When Bella and Lia met for the first time, they cuddled and played together all day long.

Lia became a perfect part of their family. She trained quickly. She never barked unnecessarily, and she loved taking long walks. After her walks she played with Bella and her toys. After her playtime, she would flop-down and take a long nap.

Before adopting Lia, Ellyn and Ken made plans to go on a fishing excursion with their friends. Their family owned a cottage on a lake. Friends and families would get together for fun-filled weekends of fishing, barbeques, and relaxing.

Once everyone arrived at the cottage, Lia was introduced to each friend. They too, FELL IN LOVE with her. Between her big brown eyes and her cute little face, each friend wanted to keep her.

Do you think Ellyn and Ken would give away their puppy?

After all the greetings and smiles, a friend shouted out, "LET THE FISHING BEGIN." "DID WE NOT COME HERE TO FISH?" yelled another friend.

After those words were spoken, out came the rowboats, oars, tackle boxes and bait. Everyone was excited to start fishing!

Lia was standing at the shoreline watching all the excitement. She seemed to be mesmerized by the ripples of waves in the water.

As Ken rowed his boat, he said, "Lia, you are going fishing with us. Come, jump into the boat." Lia jumped quickly into the boat and sat on the seat behind Ken. She was thrilled to be part of the fishing team.

Ken continued rowing his boat towards an Island in the middle of the lake.

This was the spot where most of the fish were caught. The Island was far from the shoreline. The water was deep and full of wild weeds.

"SPLASH, SPLASH" Ken quickly turned around to see what happened! **LIA WAS NOT IN THE BOAT!!** Ken started to yell, "Lia, Lia". He was very frightened! Did Lia hit her head on the side of the boat when she fell? Did Lia get caught and tangled in the weeds? If so, she would never be able to free herself. So many thoughts entered his mind. Where can Lia be? He continued looking and calling out her name. "Lia, Lia".

SUDDENLY, LIA APPEARED! She was struggling to get into the boat. Ken lifted her up and noticed a fish flapping from side to side in her mouth. Once Lia was back in the boat, she dropped the fish. The fish started flapping and jumping. Everything in the boat got wet!

"Woof-Woof" barked Lia. "Woof-Woof."

Ken was surprised! How could this tiny puppy dive into the deep water and catch a fish?

"Woof-Woof" barked Lia once again.

Do you think Ken was happy Lia caught a fish?

There were many times Ken and his friends would fish for hours and never catch anything! Yet, each time Lia dove into the water, she would always catch a fish.

"We must be doing something wrong," shouted a friend. "Lia makes us look like AMATEURS."

Another friend yelled, "If we had a fishing contest, Lia would definitely be the WINNER."

After many hours of fishing, dinner time was approaching. All the friends were looking forward to having a barbeque and playing games.

In the evening, everyone gathered around a campfire. They toasted marshmallows, made smores, told ghost stories and gazed at the moon and stars. During this time, Lia was fast asleep in Ellyn's arms. After all, this was her first fishing experience, and she was exhausted!

"LET THE FISHING CONTINUE TOMORROW MORNING," laughed a friend. Plans were now being made to meet very early the next day.

At sunrise everyone met. They were all ready for the new FISHING DAY to begin. Lia continued diving into the water. Each time she appeared, there was another fish flapping in her mouth. By this time everyone had stopped counting how many fish she caught.

By late afternoon, it was time to end the weekend. All the boats and fishing gear were being put away until the next fishing trip.

It was at that time Ellyn noticed Lia standing at the shoreline. The sun was glistening down on the lake. With breezes from the wind, it looked as though thousands of diamonds were dancing on the water.

Lia once again dove into the lake. She started swimming far out towards the Island. Ellyn yelled, "LIA, COME BACK. LIA, COME HERE, LIA COME HERE NOW!!!"

Why do you think Lia was swimming towards the Island?

When Lia heard her name, she turned around and swam back to the shoreline. She ran to Ellyn to show her what she caught. Lia had a **HUGE** fish in her mouth. This was the **LARGEST** fish Lia ever caught. The fish was much **BIGGER** than she was!

Ken, Ellyn and all their friends were amazed at Lia's fishing skills and her strength.

The **HUGE** fish was flapping and trying to get free. After everyone saw the **LARGE** fish, Lia turned around and started running back to the shoreline. She dropped the fish into the water. **THE FISH WAS NOW FREE**. He began swimming very quickly towards the Island.

"Woof-Woof" barked Lia. "Woof-Woof."

What do you think Lia was saying to the fish?

The cars were all packed and everyone was ready to leave for home. After the goodbyes, each friend headed for the road. It looked like a parade of cars driving in a straight line one by one.

Just then, a friend shouted out his opened window "What a great time we had. I cannot wait for our next fishing weekend."

Another friend yelled **"AND DON'T FORGET TO BRING LIA."**

THE END

RALPH, THE FRIENDLY GOAT

This is a true story about a goat named Ralph.

Ralph is an older goat raised on Connemara Farms in North Carolina. It was owned by a well-known poet and author, Carl Sandburg and his wife. This farm has been raising dairy goats for many years. The tradition of raising goats continues to this day. Their milk is distributed and sold throughout North Carolina and the neighboring States.

Between looking at the Blue Ridge Mountains, the green pastures, and seeing all the goats basking in the sun, the views at the farm are picture perfect.

As the goats gathered, we were amazed! It appeared each group of goats had their own story to tell!

The baby goats never left their Mommy's side. Each little goat wore a knitted sweater to keep toasty warm. They were adorable and so very cute.

The older goats slowly ventured out to see new faces in the crowd. They were not frightened to meet and greet new visitors.

The senior goats, however, stayed close to the barn. They were not friendly and just wanted to be left alone!

We noticed every goat was different! Some goats were solid colored, and some goats were multi-colored. Many goats had two different colored eyes! There were goats with horns and long goatees. Yet, some goats did not have horns, but did have short goatees. **Each one was special in his own way!**

While glancing at the goats, a particular one caught our eye! He was brown and tan with a long goatee. He was walking slowly towards us. "Baa, Baa, Baa," were the sounds coming from him. "Baa, Baa, Baa."

The goat keeper informed us, "That's Ralph. He is 15 years old. He loves to nibble on your fingers and chew your clothes. If you realize you are missing a piece of clothing from your jacket or pants, most likely Ralph ate it. He loves to be brushed and will answer you if you speak to him. He is a sweet goat. He chews and chomps constantly but will never bite." The whole time the goat keeper was talking to us, Ralph stood near us saying, "Baa, Baa, Baa."

As we were petting Ralph's head and saying "**GOODBYE**", Ralph started to circle around us. "Baa, Baa, Baa," he whispered.

The goat keeper laughed and said, "Ralph does not want you to leave! Maybe you should tell him you will see him tomorrow."

We all looked at each other when the goat keeper said those words!!!!

"**Don't be SAD, Ralph!**" We will come again tomorrow to visit you. Ralph looked up into our eyes and cried, "Baa, Baa, Baa."

Do you think a goat understands what you are saying to him?

Do you know what Ralph was thinking?

The goat keeper then said, "Ralph likes you. I think you are his new best friends." Everyone looked at each other and smiled!

We all took turns brushing Ralph's fur and telling him how handsome he looked. Each time Ralph received a compliment, we heard "Baa, Baa, Baa, Baa, Baa, Baa."

After being at the farm for most of the day, the visiting hours were soon coming to an end.

Finally, the goat keeper announced, "The farm is closing for the day. Everyone please **EXIT** through the front gates!"

Ralph looked very **UNHAPPY** as we all were leaving. "Baa, Baa, Baa," he kept repeating. He then turned around and started walking back to the barn.

"**GOODBYE RALPH**," we yelled. "We will see you tomorrow." Ralph just continued walking slowly. He did not turn to look at us!

Early the next morning we were excited to return to the farm to see Ralph! Once we arrived and Ralph heard our voices, he came to us. "Baa, Baa, Baa, Baa, Baa, Baa" were the sounds he was making.

The goat keeper looked at Ralph and said, "Ralph, your new best friends are here to see you once again. I think they are in love with you." "Baa, Baa, Baa, Baa, Baa, Baa," were the sounds we heard!

Ralph no longer looked **UNHAPPY**. He was cheerful and he started to dance around us. So many people at the farm were surprised to see a goat dancing! **"Yes, that's our RALPH, THE FRIENDLY GOAT,"** said the goat keeper. **"Baa, Baa, Baa, Baa, Baa, Baa" were the joyful sounds coming from Ralph.**

Would you like to have a goat like Ralph for a pet? If so, do you think he would love you forever?

THE MORAL OF THIS STORY IS: Always be kind to animals. When an animal feels your love and kindness, he will become your forever best friend.

THE END

THE MISSING PARAKEET

Once upon a time there was a little girl named Anne who owned a beautiful parakeet. This bird was special in many ways. From the moment Anne had him, she knew she would love him forever.

Anne was seven years old when her mom purchased a baby parakeet from a pet store for her. His feathers were yellow and green with eyes that sparkled. Anne named him Jo-Jo.

After having Jo-Jo for a few weeks, she began teaching him many tricks. His favorite trick was to sit on Anne's shoulder and tweet, tweet, tweet in her ear. He would do this continuously until he was put back in his cage.

One summer day when Anne was playing with her friends outdoors, her mom and sister, Terry, wanted to surprise her by cleaning Jo-Jo's cage. The cleaning of the cage was always done by Anne, usually on the weekend.

When Terry lifted the cage door, Jo-Jo flew out. He started circling and flying all around the bedroom. She noticed Jo-Jo was flying towards the window. She now realized the window was s till **OPENED** from the night before. She tried to distract him, but it was too late! **Suddenly, Jo-Jo was gone!** Anne's family lived in an apartment on the third floor. Surrounding the building were massive trees. Most likely Jo-Jo flew into one of them.

Both mom and Terry stood **MOTIONLESS**. They could not believe this happened! Neither one of them checked to see if the window was opened before they started to clean the cage.

Terry said, "Mom, how are we going to tell Anne her precious Jo-Jo is **MISSING?**" Mom was perplexed! She sat on the bed wondering what to do next. At that moment, she had a thought!

"Let's go, Terry. We are going to the pet store to buy Anne another parakeet. We better hurry before the pet store closes for the evening."

The manager was just about to close the store when they arrived. He directed them to the parakeet area. There were many parakeets of different colors. It looked like a rainbow of birds sitting on perches. Mom and Terry chose a bird that resembled Jo-Jo.

Do you think it was a good idea for mom and Terry to buy Anne a look alike bird?

After playing with her friends, it was time for Anne to venture home. She knew she had to clean JoJo's cage and feed him. She also planned on teaching him a new trick.

Once she arrived home, she said "Hi" to her mom and walked into her bedroom. **SHE WAS SHOCKED AT WHAT SHE SAW**!!! "You are not my Jo-Jo! You are not my bird! What are you doing here! Tears started rolling down her pretty face.

"Mommy, mommy," she yelled. Both mom and Terry ran into Anne's bedroom. They did not know what to expect!

Through her tears Anne cried, "Mommy this is not my Jo-Jo! What did you do with my Jo-Jo? Where is he?" Her mom tried to kiss and hug her daughter, but Anne pulled away. She did not want a kiss or hug; she wanted her Jo-Jo back.

Terry looked at her little sister and said, "We wanted to surprise you by cleaning Jo-Jo's cage while you were playing with your friends. When I opened the cage door, Jo-Jo flew out. He started to circle and fly around the bedroom. He was flying towards the window! I realized we never checked to see if the window was opened or closed from the night before. I tried to prevent him from flying out, but it was too late. Anne, I am so sorry!"

With a painful stare Anne said, "So you both tried to **TRICK** me by getting me another bird!!! Did you think I would not know my Jo-Jo? Did you think I would not know my own pet?" She was so upset that she kept repeating the same words over and over. Everlasting tears were still rolling down her little face.

Mom kissed her little girl's wet cheeks, and with all her love, she said, "Anne, we did not try to **TRICK** you by buying you a new bird. We knew how **UNHAPPY** you would be when we told you Jo-Jo was **missing.** We did not want you to come home and see an empty cage. We honestly thought you would feel better having a new bird."

Anne looked at her mom and said, "This new bird is not my Jo-Jo. I will **NEVER, NEVER** like or love him. I don't want him. Take him back to where you got him!"

With sweet words spoken Terry said, "Anne, give this new bird a chance. Maybe one day your feelings will change, and you will grow to love or like him." Anne replied, **"NO, I NEVER WILL WANT OR LOVE** this new bird."

Mom and Terry now wondered if they did the right thing by getting Anne another parakeet. They felt sorry for this new bird because they knew he would **NEVER** be loved or wanted.

With more tears rolling down Anne's face, she said, "Mommy, I want my Jo-Jo back. Maybe if we leave the window open all the time, he will fly back to us." "What a good idea," said Terry. "Yes, we will leave the window opened day and night until Jo-Jo comes back home to you." Anne looked at her sister and tried to smile.

Many times, Anne's family would look up into the trees hoping to spot Jo-Jo, but his coloring blended in with the leaves making it impossible to ever see him.

Anne kept telling herself that Jo-Jo would come back someday. Each night when she said her bedtime prayers, she asked God to protect Jo-Jo and please bring him back home to her. She knew God heard her prayers and listened to every word she said.

Many weeks passed and now **Summertime** was coming to an end. The leaves on the trees were changing and the weather was much cooler. With **Fall** arriving soon, Anne wondered if Jo-Jo was safe, was he hungry, or was he cold? Once again, she asked God to keep Jo-Jo free from harm and please bring him back home to her.

After Fall ended, **Wintertime** arrived. There were predictions of a bad snowstorm with high winds heading their way. The temperature was dropping rapidly, and everyone was told to stay indoors.

Hearing the bad weather predictions throughout the day, mom thought it would be better to close the window for the evening; but Anne decided to leave the window **OPENED**. She did not care about the brutal cold, winds or the snowstorm. Her only thoughts were on Jo-Jo and asking God to protect him during the night.

Do you think Anne made a good choice by keeping the window open during the bad snowstorm?

By bedtime, it was extremely cold. Anne gathered many blankets to keep warm. Once she was comfortable, she said her bedtime prayers. After saying her prayers, she closed her eyes and dozed off. She dreamed of Jo-Jo sitting on her shoulder and tweeting in her ear.

Do you think this was a dream, or was Jo-Jo really with her?

The next morning Anne's mom went to check on her little girl. Anne was snuggled under all the blankets and fast asleep. It looked as though she was having a sweet dream and there was a smile on her face.

Watching her daughter sleep, mom thought she heard a baby tweet. A second later, she heard another baby tweet. "Oh my," What do we have here?" she said. **SHE DID NOT BELIEVE WHAT SHE WAS LOOKING AT!!!**

"Anne, wake up! Anne wake up! All your prayers have been answered!" said her mom.

Anne was toasty warm and did not want to be awakened yet. Her mom repeated, **"Anne wake up! There is a big surprise waiting for you! Look who is here!"**

As comfortable as she was, Anne started to move the blankets to one side. She tried sitting up when she heard a tweet, tweet, tweet. At first, she thought she was dreaming. ALL OF A SUDDEN, she heard another tweet, tweet, tweet. She looked down and there he was. He was sitting on all her blankets staying warm and cozy.

"Jo-Jo, you came back. Jo-Jo, you did come back to me!" screamed Anne. She lifted her little bird and held him close to her heart. She looked at him and said, "Jo-Jo, God answered **ALL** my prayers. I am so **HAPPY!** God brought you back to me. Jo-Jo, I missed you so very much."

Now that Jo-Jo was finally back home with Anne, it was time to close the opened window. As Terry walked near the window, she turned to glance at her little sister. Anne looked so content and happy. There were no more tears rolling down her face. **All her prayers had been answered**.

Once Terry closed the window, she wondered, "How did this tiny bird fly through the gusty winds, the heavy snow and the bitter cold? How did Jo-Jo ever find his way back home to Anne? How was this possible?"

At that moment, she knew this was a **miracle**. She then walked over to Anne's bedside and gave her little sister a **BIG HUG AND KISS**. Everyone was so **HAPPY** Jo-Jo was finally back home with them!

The moral of this story is: Always believe in the power of prayer and miracles. **MIRACLES HAPPEN EVERY DAY.**

THE END

Printed in the United States
by Baker & Taylor Publisher Services